Making Music

Banging

Angela Aylmore

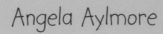

Heinemann LIBRARY

Little Nippers

www.heinemann.co.uk/library
Visit our website to find out more information about **Heinemann Library** books.

To order:
☎ Phone 44 (0) 1865 888066
🖹 Send a fax to 44 (0) 1865 314091
🖥 Visit the Heinemann Bookshop at www.heinemann.co.uk/library to browse our catalogue and order online.

First published in Great Britain by Heinemann Library, Halley Court, Jordan Hill, Oxford OX2 8EJ, part of Harcourt Education.
Heinemann is a registered trademark of Harcourt Education Ltd.

Editorial: Kathy Peltan and Kate Bellamy
Design: Jo Hinton-Malivoire and Bigtop
Picture Research: Ruth Blair
Production: Severine Ribierre

Originated by Chroma Graphics (Overseas) Pte. Ltd
Printed and bound in China by South China Printing Company

ISBN 0 431 08821 7 (hardback)
10 09 08 07 06
10 9 8 7 6 5 4 3 2 1

ISBN 0 431 08826 8 (paperback)
09 08 07 06 05
10 9 8 7 6 5 4 3 2 1

British Library Cataloguing in Publication Data
Aylmore, Angela
Making Music: Banging
786.9
A full catalogue record for this book is available from the British Library.

Acknowledgements
The publishers would like to thank the following for permission to reproduce photographs: Alamy p. **15**; Corbis pp. **4b**, **5a**, **6**, **18**; Harcourt Education pp. **14** (Gareth Boden), **4a**, **5b** (Trevor Clifford), **13** (Peter Evans), **18** (Chris Honeywell), **7**, **8**, **9**, **10**, **11**, **12**, **16**, **17**, **19**, **20**, **21**, **22-23** (Tudor Photography).

Cover photograph of a girl playing a drum, reproduced with permission of Harcourt Education/Tudor Photography.

Every effort has been made to contact copyright holders of any material reproduced in this book. Any omissions will be rectified in subsequent printings if notice is given to the publishers.

The paper used to print this book comes from sustainable resources.

Contents

Let's make music!

We can make music by banging!

Ravi **bangs** the drum.

Crash go the cymbals!

Tom hits his xylophone.

The triangle goes **ting ting**.

Play the drum

Can you play the drum?

Bang it **hard**. Make it **loud**.

Boom!

6

Tap it **gently**.
Keep it **soft**.

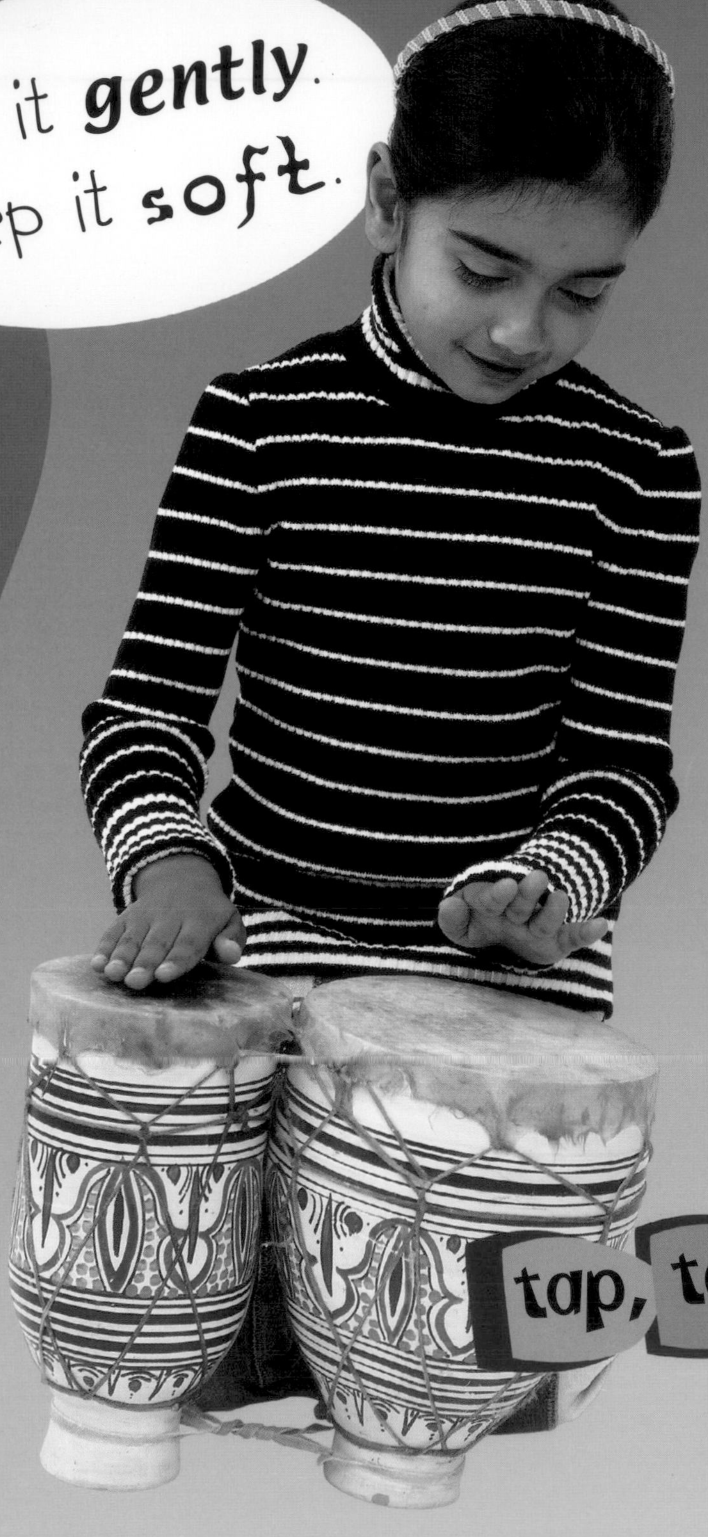

Low and high

Let's play the glockenspiel.

Hit a low note.

Dong!

Make your own

Can you make a drum?

My drum is made from an old box.

Boom!

Can you play a pan?

Bang

Slow, slow. Faster and faster.

What are they?

These drums are from Indonesia.
They are called bonang.

A bonang sounds like a gong.

15

Play the cymbals

Bash the cymbals together!

Crash!

Tap them gently.

Ping

Keep in time

click-clack

castanets

The castanets click-clack.

The dancer's feet tip-tap.

tip-tap

One, two.
One, two.

Can you march
with the beat?

Listen carefully

What can you hear?

ting

triangle

maracas

violin

recorder

What makes that sound?

It's the triangle!

All together now!

Let's all play together!

ting

clip-clop

23

Index

Notes for adults

Making Music provides children with an opportunity to think about sound and the different ways instruments can be played to create music. The concept of volume, rhythm, speed and pitch are introduced, and children are encouraged to think about how controlling their movements can create different sounds when they play instruments. The following Early Learning Goals are relevant to this series:

Creative development - music
• explore the different sounds of instruments and learn how sounds can be changed
Knowledge and understanding of the world
• look closely at similarities, differences, patterns and change
• show an interest in why things happen and how things work
Physical development
• respond to rhythm by means of gesture and movement
• manage body to create intended movements

This book explores the different ways of creating music by banging. It includes a range of instruments, some with pitch and some without, and looks at different ways that instruments can be hit to create different sounds, by using sticks or hands, by hitting hard or tapping gently, and by banging quickly or slowly.

Follow-up activities

• With their eyes closed, ask the children to identify the instruments that you play.

• Can the children use their instruments to represent different feelings and emotions? For example, quick high notes on the xylophone might be 'happy', while slow low notes might be 'sad'.

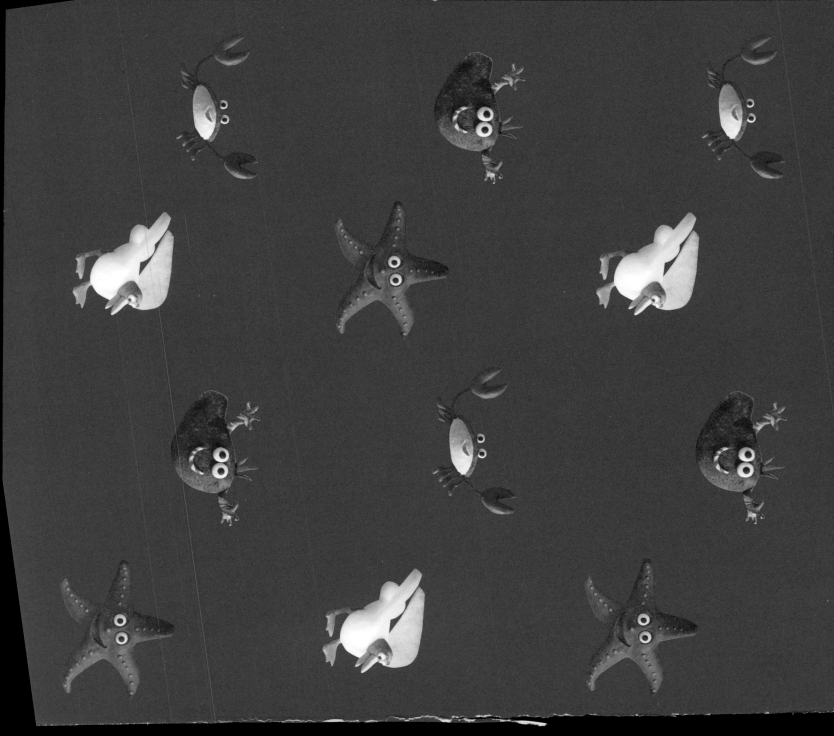